DEATH VALLEY
A Day in the Desert

BY
NANCY SMILER LEVINSON
ILLUSTRATED BY
DIANE DAWSON HEARN

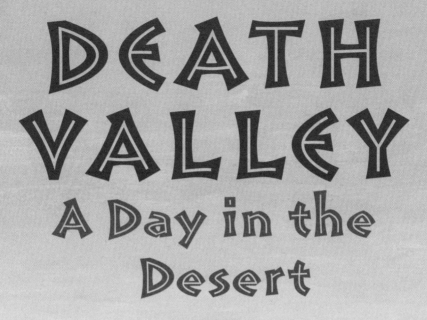

Holiday House / NEW YORK

Thanks are due to Death Valley National Park for cooperation, and
to Roger Brandt, Park Ranger; Pat Compton, Visitor Services;
and Dick Anderson, Environmental Specialist, for their special assistance.
James Murakami, Research Associate, Atmospheric Science Department,
University of California, Los Angeles, was also helpful
in the preparation of this book.

Library of Congress Cataloging-in-Publication Data
Levinson, Nancy Smiler.
Death Valley: a day in the desert / by Nancy Smiler Levinson;
illustrated by Diane Dawson Hearn.—1st ed.
p. cm.
Summary: Describes the desert habitat of Death Valley and
the plants and animals that live there.
ISBN 0-8234-1566-X (hc.)
1. Natural history—Death Valley (Calif. and Nev.)—Juvenile literature.
2. Desert ecology—Death Valley (Calif. and Nev.)—Juvenile literature.
[1. Natural History—Death Valley (Calif. and Nev.) 2. Desert ecology—
Death Valley (Calif. and Nev.)
3. Ecology—Death Valley (Calif. and Nev.)]
I. Hearn, Diane Dawson, ill. II. Title.
QH104.5.D4 L48 2001
508.794'87—dc21
00-023305

kangaroo rat

For Eve Bunting,
who led the way
N. S. L.

With thanks
to Jonathan Kingston
D. D. H.

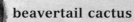

beavertail cactus

barrel cactus

darkling beetle

kit fox

scorpion

4

There is a desert
in California.
It is called
Death Valley.

coyote

A desert is dry land
and dry air.

Scott's
oriole

rabbitbrush

The Arctic and Antarctic are
deserts, too. They are cold,
polar deserts.

sagebrush

chuckwalla

Most deserts are hot.
Death Valley is one of the
hottest of all.
How hot is it?
In summer,
the temperature can rise to
125 degrees!

red-tailed hawk

9

desert spiny lizard

The ground gets even hotter.
It gets up to 200 degrees.
That would melt the rubber
on a pair of sneakers.
That's hot!

What can you see in Death Valley?
There are mountains and rocks,
salt flats and sand.
There are bushes and cactus plants,
but no trees are growing.
And there is bright sunlight.

salt flats

sage

desert tarantula

mouse

beehive
cactus

13

Indian ricegrass

roadrunner

Hardly any rain falls in Death Valley.
Mountains keep out moist air
and low rain clouds.

arrowweed

desert
holly

The air is so dry,
the soil crumbles
and turns to sand.

rough
harvester
ants

15

The wind blows
the sand into big hills.
They are called sand dunes.
It also carves rocks
into many shapes.

sidewinder

16

Mojave yucca

tamarisk

desert trumpet

Plants and wildflowers
live in Death Valley.
Only tough plants can survive.

The creosote bush holds water
in its leaves, stems, and roots.
It can hold the water for months.

19

Mormon cricket

gopher snake

20

A barrel cactus can save a life.
If a thirsty traveler gets lost,
he can cut off the cactus top.
Then he can drink the pulpy
juice inside.

rock wren

Small animals live in Death Valley.
Pocket mice and kangaroo rats
live in tunnels deep in the ground.

white-tailed
antelope
squirrel

crescent
milk
vetch

pocket
mouse

beavertail
cactus

big
free-tailed
bats

desert cottontail

23

bobcat

At night the desert air cools fast.
That is when animals come out
to search for food.

kit fox

wild burros

red-spotted
toad

killdeer

great horned owl

Death Valley mammals,
reptiles, and birds
find water in creeks
and in springs under the ground.

spiny softshell

Where does the water come from?
Once or twice a year in Death Valley,
the sky turns dark.
The clouds burst.

Rain rushes down in a wall of water.
It rains for only an hour or two.
That is enough to keep the desert
alive.

Common Death Valley Animals and Plants

big
free-tailed bat

kangaroo rat

bobcat

MAMMALS

ground squirrel

coyote

AMPHIBIANS

ARACHNIDS

red-spotted
toad

scorpion

desert tarantula

BIRDS

roadrunner

great horned owl

raven

REPTILES

chuckwalla

sidewinder

desert tortoise

PLANTS

Joshua tree

Mojave yucca

More about Death Valley

—Death Valley National Park is part of the Mojave Desert.

—The highest air temperature recorded there was 134 degrees.

—Rainfall averages less than two inches a year. Most rain evaporates into the air.

—The temperature averages 65 degrees on winter days. At night it drops to about 40 degrees.

—Hundreds of species of mammals, reptiles, and birds live there.

—The lowest elevation in the Western hemisphere is in Death Valley. It is called Badwater and lies 282 feet below sea level.

—Nearly one million people visit Death Valley every year.